BIG

DATA

*A Complete Guide to the Basic
Concepts in Data Science, Cyber
Security, Analytics and Metrics*

TABLE OF CONTENTS

Introduction 1

Chapter One: Big Data and Data Science 2

History of Data Science.. 3

Definition of Data Science 4

Who is a Data Scientist? 4

How Data Scientists Increase the Worth of a Business............. 6

The Technique of Data Science 8

Impacts of Data Science 8

Importance of Data Science 8

Programming Languages Every Data Scientist Should Know ... 10

The Data Science Process 13

The Future of Data Science as a Carrier Choice 18

Chapter Two: Cyber Security 21

Introduction.. 21

Most Common Cybersecurity Threats....................... 23

Impacts of Cyber Attacks on Business....................... 29

How can Cyber-Attacks be Reduced?........................ 31

Creating responsiveness of cyber-security within an
organization.. 32

Investing in cyber safety and cyber-security backup 33

Keeping up to date with all of the safety arrangements
and testing the security measures regularly 33

Chapter Three: Cyber Technology 34

Features that Must be Present in a
Cyber Technology Platform 37

Best Cybersecurity Practices for Businesses 39

The Future of Cyber Security 46

How AI (Artificial Intelligence) will shape the future of Cyber. 47

Chapter Four: Analytics and Metrics for Big Data 51

Analytics and Metrics of Big Data and Data Science 51

Cybersecurity Analytics and Metrics 53

Conclusion **62**

Bibliography **66**

Introduction

Welcome to the world of Big Data. This book will give you a complete insight into the basic concepts in Data Science, Cyber Security, Analytics, and Metrics. The first section of the book will describe the concepts of Big Data. Everyone knows that data and information in the current technical and business world are crucial. Big data refers to large amounts of data sized data in structured and unstructured arrangements that affect business on a daily basis. The amount of data does not matter. Data affects the businesses and organization of that business. Big data is examined for insights that generate better choices and planned corporate changes. Data science is a vast subject that uses technical approaches, procedures, processes, and schemes to get information from many sources.

The second portion of the book will describe the concepts of Cyber Security. Cyber-security is the field of protecting processors, servers, systems, grids, and information from malevolent attacks. Cybersecurity is also known as IT security. This guide will describe the different categories of cybersecurity in detail, the methods, procedures used, and how the systems are protected.

The final portion of this guide will deal with analytics and metrics for big data. Analytics and metrics define the methods in which the data is converted into ideas that are applied across businesses and corporations. This book will also discuss performance analytics and metrics of big data, data science, and cybersecurity.

Chapter One

Big Data and Data Science

Nowadays, we all live in a world of information and data. In this digital age, Data is present everywhere. The digital data is increasing at a fast rate. According to statistics, the data gets multiplied by two times every two years (Vaidya, 2019). In a company or business, data is considered as a primary asset. The process of data processing includes concepts of data science, data analysis, and big data.

Some years ago, data was produced only by the work-force working in companies. The data that was generated before used to have some specific structure. It usually consisted of employee records, delivery information, the amount of money generated and hiring information, etc. With the advancements in technology, now, the data comes in large volumes and in many different formats. Data is produced in large volumes by networking, databases, and the new technology of cloud computing. A flood of new information is forming every day. Large amounts of data come in an unstructured format. One common example of unstructured or semi-structured data is the data used during the transaction of payment (Big data Basics). An innovative age of Big Data is evolving. The effects of the corporate sector and government organizations are enormous. Large databases are studied and analyzed to find new patterns of data. This extracted data is used for decision-making capability in business corporations. Currently, data scientists are searching for new ways to make new uses of large databases.

To forecast the data and information, everybody needs data experts. The fields of Data Science and Big Data hold the vital key to the future of the data field. The field of data science is significant for improved advertising and promotion. Businesses are utilizing data and information to examine their advertising plans and generate better commercial advertisements.

The demand and requirement for data experts are growing so rapidly that it was predicted that by 2018, there would have been a 50% gap in the availability of data experts versus the requirement (Thompson). The increasing significance of data science has led to the development and prominence of data scientists. These data specialists are currently an essential part of trademarks, industries, community organizations, and non-profit administrations. The data experts work determinedly to organize the enormous quantity of information and regulate appropriate designs and strategies in the data. In this way, the data can be efficiently used to understand future objectives and ideas.

History of Data Science

The beginning of the field of data science can be found around fifty years back when it was used as a substitute for computer science in 1960 by Peter Naur. During the year 1974, Peter printed a book called "Concise Survey of Computer Methods." In this book, he described the term "Data Science" in its review of the modern information and data processing methods (Data Science and Its Growing Importance).

Définition of Data Science

Currently, Data science is a major field. In this field, the data scientists create such processes in which useful knowledge is extracted from larger databases and collections of data. Data Science can be considered as a continuation of fields such as Data mining and analytical analysis. Data science practices numerous concepts and methods that belong to other scientific areas such as information technology, arithmetic calculations, statistics, computer science, and software engineering. Some of the basic techniques used in Data Science include prospect models, concepts of artificial intelligence, signal processing, information mining, arithmetical learning, databases, cloud computing, design recognition, and computer programming. Data science is not limited to the field of big data - big data is a different area because it provides resolutions that are more dedicated to formatting and pre-processing the statistics and information rather than evaluating the data.

Who is a Data Scientist?

A Data scientist is defined as a computer expert, database and program writer, corrective expert, supervisor, and expert annotator. These people are very significant for the effective organization of the latest data assembly. Their main job is to plan the inventive review and examination for the data to be used in a correct and operative way by organizations. Without the proficiency and knowledge of specialists who turn the latest technology into actionable understanding, big data is nothing. Currently, numerous organizations are adopting big data to unlock its power. This is aggregating the worth of a data scientist who is an expert with the technical know-how to take actionable insights out of a mountain of data. A data scientist is capable of doing three tasks:

- Data Analysis

- Data Modeling.

- The engineering and prototyping of processes.

These three above mentioned tasks describe the working life cycle of a typical data science project.

A Data Scientist also performs the following tasks:

- Linking fresh and dissimilar information to propose products that meet the ambitions and objectives of their marked customers.

- Using sensor information to identify climate surroundings and redirect supply chains.

- Discovering the deceptions and irregularities in the marketplace. Data scientists are skilled in recognizing data that is prominent in some way. After this, they create geometric net paths and big data practices to project fraud tendency models and use them to generate alerts that will ensure timely replies when uncommon data is found.

- Improve the swiftness at which information sets can be retrieved and combined.

- Recognize the finest and innovative method to utilize the Internet so that the marketers can use the prospects in a complete way.

How Data Scientists Increase the Worth of a Business

Data specialists or data scientists can add value to a business as well as they will increase the assets of the business. Following are some ways in which a data scientist can add worth to business:

● The managing team can make improved choices:

A skilled data scientist is expected to be a trustworthy consultant and planning partner to the establishment's higher management by safeguarding that the workforce makes the most out of their methodical abilities.

● Guiding activities based on the latest trends:

Data scientists inspect and search the establishment's data. After a proper inspection, they will recommend and suggest definite activities that will aid in improving the establishment's presentation, improve customer involvement, and eventually take the company towards success.

● Challenging the workforce to accept best strategies and emphasize on problems that are important:

The duties of a data scientist include safeguarding that the workforce is acquainted and familiar with the establishment's operating environment. Data scientists will organize the people of the company to achieve using live demos of the operative use of the computer systems to mine insights and determine the acts that need to be done. When all the people understand the system capabilities, their emphasis could be changed toward addressing important challenges of the company.

- Making choices with the evidence of information:

When different data scientists are working in an organization, data collection, and investigation from numerous sources does not involve great risks. Data scientists construct models using current data that creates a range of possible activities. It leads to business learning new paths that will get the finest corporate results.

- Refining of target viewers:

Almost all companies have one or more sources of client data that is collected. The significance of data science is based on the capability to take current data that is not essentially valuable and uniting it with other information to produce understandings a business can utilize to study about its clients and viewers. Data scientists can assist with the identification of the vital collection of data regarding a company's audience with precision.

- Hiring the right people for the company:

By extracting the large amount of data that is available, processing for curriculum vitae and applications can be done easily. The employment team can make quicker and more precise choices.

- Testing every decision that the company makes:

After applying necessary changes to the data and extracting information, it is necessary to test every decision. After this, the data scientists will measure how the changes that they applied changed the business processes.

The Technique of Data Science

Data science highlights the usage of universal approaches for business problems without altering its application. This technique is different from a traditional approach because it is inclined to concentrate on giving solutions that are precise to specific areas of the business. Data science provides a standard solution to all the business's problems. Data science is valued in businesses and the IT industry.

Impacts of Data Science

Currently, data science has its effect in many fields. These fields include both educational and applied engineering domains such as machine learning, language recognition, and economy. It is also used in fields such as medicine, health informatics, and healthcare. The development and expansion of any brand are affected by it. It offers large amounts of intellect about customers and operations by using techniques such as data extraction and data examination.

Importance of Data Science

The importance of data science can be understood from the following points:

- Data science supports different companies to understand their clients in an improved and empowered way. Customers are a vital part of any company, and they have the power of making or breaking a business. Data science provides a personalized way to companies for dealing with their customers. Therefore it ensures the company's power to grow steadily.

- The companies can utilize their customer's data in a proper manner. Companies can share their own stories with their focused viewers to create an enriched company connect.

- Data science is reachable to nearly all divisions of the IT realm. A huge amount of information is present in the world today, and operating this data in a correct manner can cause success and failure for businesses and organizations.

- The primary advantage of data science is that it finds and produces results. These results can be used in any field regarding tourism, healthcare, and learning, etc.

- Big Data is an innovative field that is frequently rising and developing. Many techniques and tools are being established on an ordered basis. Big data is serving organizations to resolve difficult problems in IT and resource administration in an operational and planned way.

- Data science helps in delivering significant products to clients. One great benefit of data science is that the companies can discover where their end products are in most demand and where they sell best. It can assist in delivering the correct end products at the time when products are needed the most.

- The marketing sector of companies can understand their viewers in detail. This information will help them to generate the best customer experiences.

Programming Languages Every Data Scientist Should Know

Data science is a diverse field to work on. It uses both quantifiable talents and progressive statistical analysis with actual program design ability. Numerous programming languages are required in data science. Data science involves the usage of scientific procedures and approaches to examine and draw deductions from this information. Particular programming languages are considered for the role of data scientists. Many programming languages are used in the development of software and application development. Software design for Data Science varies from general software development. It supports to pre-practice, examine, and create forecasts from data. These data-focused programming languages have the capability of processing algorithms that are suitable for the particulars of Data Science. It is a necessity for data scientists who own the mandatory skills for becoming an expert in the field of data science. Before attaining proficiency, an ambitious Data Scientist needs to be able to make the correct choice about the kind of programming language necessary for the work of data science. The following is the list of some programming languages every Data Scientist should know about:

Python

Python is a tremendously widespread, generic, and dynamic and extensively used programming language among data science professionals. It is an easy high programming language. The nature of Python language is versatile. It is easier in both reading and writing. Its code is easily readable. While dealing with complex problems, the readability of this language makes it the choice of many data scientists. Implementing solutions is easier in this

10

language. It quickly interfaces with algorithms designed for data science, therefore, making it the first choice of data scientists. Python programmers are in great demand currently in the IT market. Python has appeared as one of the greatest standard selections for Data Science due to its smooth knowledge arc and valuable libraries.

R Language

It is the most commonly used language in data science. The source code of R language is available. The environment of the R language is used for arithmetical calculations and visuals. R language is maintained by the R Foundation for Statistical Computing (L, 2019). Arithmetic calculations and visuals are in great demand among employers in the field of artificial intelligence and data science. R language brings many numerical models, and many data analysts have created their applications in the R language. The "Community R set library" covers more than 8,000 systems contributed sets. R is perfect for statistical tasks. Linear algebra's complex tasks are easily handled by this programming language. It also provides smooth database connectivity. It is, therefore, a perfect selection for data scientists.

Java

Java is a very general and popular language. It runs on the Java Virtual Machine. This language is supported by Oracle. It permits manageability between different platforms. Java is commonly known as the pillar or foundation of the programming stack. Java Software Engineers and Java System architects are in high demand for data science organizations. Java is considered a good choice by data scientists

Scala

Scala is an extension of Java programming language. It provides functional programming as well as object-oriented programming. It can be used with Apache Spark, which is a big data platform. This conjunction with a big data platform makes it an ideal choice for data scientists when they want to deal with a huge amount of data. Scala is completely operational with the Java language. Scala offers parallel processing, and it is one of the highlighting features of Scala. This language is recommended for experts, but it is not recommended for beginners.

SQL

SQL can be considered as the core of data science. A data scientist must be an expert in this language. It is used to extract data from relational databases by querying the information. SQL is basically an old language. Being a skilled expert in SQL could be the main advantage for Artificial intelligence professionals and data science specialists. SQL is the best-desired skill for almost all establishments. SQL demonstrates a vital part in Data Science as it supports the following functions such as updating, enquiring, and altering databases. SQL is essential for specific roles in Data Science. Familiarity with SQL is highly essential because the mining and alternation of the data from the database are possible with the help of SQL. SQL has a declarative syntax, and therefore it is easier to read and write.

Julia

For developing the best results regarding scientific computing, Julia is the best option. Julia is a new language. It has fast performance, and it is simple at the same time. Wherever arithmetic operations are required, Julia's language is preferred. It solves highly complex mathematical and arithmetical problems quickly; therefore, it is favored by data scientists. Nowadays, Julia is known as the most used language in artificial intelligence. Julia's language is also used for risk analytics.

Matlab

Matlab is an industrialized language, and it is approved by MathWorks. It is a fast and stable language. Matlab guarantees concrete algorithms for arithmetical calculation. It is used in the academic world and the IT industry. Matlab is considered the best language for arithmeticians and experts that work with particular mathematical requirements such as signal dispensation, image dispensation, and matrix algebra. It is used in statistical applications. Due to its mathematical processing capability, it is used in data science.

The Data Science Process

The data science process involves solving problems related to data science. There is a framework of data science that is followed during the project life cycle. Certain key skills and requirements are present in the complete project life cycle of data science. Data scientists analyze enormous sets of seemingly dissimilar data to reveal astonishing insights in the field. The procedure they use is a secret to most individuals outside the circle of data science. The following are the detailed steps required to solve a particular problem in the scenario of data science:

13

- **Consider the problem:**

The first action a data scientist takes before solving a problem is to describe precisely what the problem is. Data scientists have to be able to decipher data queries into something over which action can be taken. A data scientist will get vague responses from individuals who have certain issues. A data scientist will have to get the instinct to change rare responses into actionable results.

- **Gather the data**

The second stage of data science development is very simple. In this step, the data scientists gather the data that they require for data science from obtainable data sources. During this step, the data scientists must query the databases by consuming their practical skills such as MySQL to gather the data. Data experts will obtain data in file arrangements such as Microsoft Excel etc. If the data experts are utilizing programming languages like R or Python, they will have access to precise packages that can read statistics from these data sources right into the data science algorithms and programs. Data experts gather data from databases as well as by connecting to web APIs. The most basic way of getting information is directly from the files. Some websites allow the use of their Web APIs to gather their data.

For the tasks mentioned above, a data expert will need particular expertise. This expertise will include the management of databases. To get big data groups, a data scientist will use distributed storage such as Spark or Apachae Hadoop.

• Scrubbing the data

After gaining the data and relevant information, the next instant thing to do is the cleaning and scrubbing of the data. This procedure is to clean and strain the data. If the information is unfiltered and inappropriate, then the effects of the inquiry and analysis will not make any sense.

During this procedure, the data is converted from one arrangement to another. It is recommended to combine everything into one consistent arrangement. For example, if you have data in different Excel files, then it is suggested to combine all the Excel files into one excel file containing all the data. Scrubbing the data also includes the job of mining and substituting values. If it is found that there are lost data groups or the data appears to be non-values, a data expert substitutes the values accordingly. The data needs to be divided, combined, and extracted properly. This procedure is used for cleaning up the data, eliminating what is not required anymore, substituting what is lost, and regulating the format over which all the data is collected.

For doing the above-mentioned processes, a data expert will need a grasp of a good programming language for scrubbing the data. For the management of larger data groups, it is required to have skills in Hadoop and Spark.

• Exploring the Data

The third step is the examination of the extracted data. Typically, in a business or corporate environment, the managers just give a group of data to the experts, and they will study the data. The data scientists will figure out the corporate questions and alter the information into a data science query. To achieve this, an exploration of the data is essential. Data experts need to review the data and their characteristics. Different types of data require different actions. In the next step data, experts calculate expressive statistics to get features and examine important variables. Examining important variables frequently is done with the help of the association.

For the above-mentioned task, a data scientist needs to have information and abilities in inferential data and information visualization.

● **Modeling the data**

This is the 4th stage in the data science process, and it is considered the most important stage in the entire data science project lifecycle. To get to this stage, the cleaning of data and exploration of data are extremely important as those two phases lead to making useful and meaningful models. Firstly, decrease the dimensionality of your information group. All the values are not vital to forecasting the model. Just consider the applicable values that give an estimate of the results. Many tasks can be performed using modeling. Regular expressions and predictions are used for predicting future values. The evaluation total is carried out after the modeling process.

For the above tasks, both supervised and unsupervised algorithms are required.

- **Understanding of the data**

This is the final step of the entire data science process. This step is the most crucial step in the entire process. The prognostic control of a model is present in its skill to generalize. A data scientist will describe a model based on the model's capacity to simplify hidden forthcoming data. Understandable data means the appearance of data to a non-technical person. This final step gives the results to deliver a solution to the business questions that were asked when the project was first started. In this process, the actionable understandings are offered through the data science process. Actionable understandings are key outcomes that demonstrate how data science can deal with projecting analytics and later prescriptive investigations. Data experts need to envision the conclusions and keep them focused in correspondence with the corporate questions. It is vital to present the results in a proper way. The results should be useful to the business.

For the above-mentioned tasks, data scientists need to have a robust business area understanding to show the results in such a way that it provides answers to the business questions.

The above mentioned 5 steps demonstrate the life cycle of a data science project. Every data scientist follows these 5 steps to answer questions related to the field of data science.

The Future of Data Science as a Carrier Choice

The job of data scientist offers a bright career. It has continuing influence in the IT market, and it delivers prospects for individuals who learn data science to offer valued contributions to their businesses and societies at great scale. Following are some reasons why Data Science is a great career choice for the future:

- **Businesses Struggle for the management of their Data**

  Businesses gather statistics and data from clients in the form of electronic transactions, web connections, etc. Data scientists have the opportunity to support companies in order to make an advancement with the information they collect. It makes them make better business decisions.

- **Data Privacy Rules increase the demand for Data Scientists**

  In May 2018, the General Data Protection Regulation (GDPR) was implemented for nations in the European Union (Methews, 2019). The GDPR improved the dependence businesses have on data scientists. It is due to the necessity for actual real-time analysis and storage of the data. It ensures that businesses comprehend how they stock the information and where they store the data properly. Currently, individuals are reasonably more cautious about providing data to companies than individuals from previous generations. Individuals are knowledgeable that data hacking can happen, and individuals have to face severe penalties. Businesses cannot treat their data carelessly. The GDPR data privacy guidelines are only the start. Data scientists can assist the businesses greatly in the use of data in a proper way along with the coherence of Data Privacy rules given by the GDPR.

• The field of Data Science is continuously Growing

Jobs without development potential remain stagnant. Data science seems to have plentiful prospects to progress over many years. It is continuously evolving, and it is great news for individuals wanting to come into this innovative field. One minor change likely to emerge soon is that data science job titles will get more specific. An individual employed as a data scientist at one business is not essentially doing similar work as another person in that same job at a different business. Individuals learning for data science jobs can begin to specify and do the tasks that are most significant to them.

• A Surprising amount of Data Growth

Data is created on a daily basis. The exponential progress of data that is observed since the start of the digital age is not predicted to slow down. The future will bring an ever-growing flood of data. The new information and data will be utilized for better data science models, and it will give rise to improved and innovative prototypes for data analysis along with original and groundbreaking use cases of data. Data creation is on an upsurge, and the data scientists should be present to deal with the data efficiently and effectively.

• High Probability of Career Progression Prospects

LinkedIn lately chose data scientists as a capable career in 2019. LinkedIn also observed the probability that individuals could get upgrades as data scientists, and it gave this job a career progression score of nine out of 10 (Methews, 2019). LinkedIn's deductions propose that companies are expected to retain data scientists on their IT teams for a long time.

Chapter Two

Cyber Security

Cybersecurity is the training of shielding computer systems, set-ups, and programs from digital hacking attacks. These cyber-attacks are typically aimed at retrieving, altering, and destroying data along with extracting money from computer users. It also includes disturbing usual business procedures.

Introduction

Cybercrime is a global problem. This problem has been ruling the news bulletins for years. It is a danger to the security of an individual, and it is an even larger danger to huge global businesses, banks, and administrations. Cybersecurity is the body of skills, procedures, and practices intended to defend nets, electronic devices, databases, and information from attack, robbery, harm, alteration, or unauthorized entry. Cybersecurity can be defined as the set of values and practices intended to defend our IT resources and virtual material against all kinds of external threats. Nowadays, everybody uses the internet, and the general computer operators are nearly unaware of the fact that how the random bits of 1 and 0 can cause security risks to the computers. This ignorant nature of computer user causes golden opportunities for hackers. With so many opportunities, the hackers, typically known as black hat hackers, create malicious codes, and they explore the vulnerabilities in the computers. Like all other kinds of innovations around us, Cyber-attacks are also evolving and becoming innovative in the nature of the attack. With time, hackers are becoming cleverer and more inventive with malicious software. They improve the methods of bypassing virus scanning software and firewalls. Therefore some kind of procedure to defend users against all of these cyber-attacks should be present. This procedure will ensure that the user data will be protected. Cybersecurity defines a set of methods that are used to defend the reliability of networks, computer programs, and information from external attacks and harm.

Computer security includes both cyber and physical security. These two types of securities are utilized by companies to defend against illicit access to information centers and other electronic systems. Information security is a subdivision of cybersecurity. The usage of cybersecurity can support in avoiding cyber-attacks, information breaches, and incidents such as identity theft. Cybersecurity can also assist in risk management. Usually, computer users save themselves from three different kinds of unauthorized accesses. These include unauthorized access to the data, unauthorized deletion of the data without any warning, and unauthorized modification. Cybersecurity deals with the availability, integrity, and confidentiality of the data. In short, the term cybersecurity prevents the sensitive data of the end-user from being falling into the wrong hands.

Cybersecurity is the safety of systems connected to the internet, hardware, computer programs, and information from hacking. The cyber-world is connected to technology. The technology comprises computer systems, net, software programs, and information. The word "security" is related to safety. It further includes systems safety, network safety, application safety, and data security. These skills, procedures, and practices can also be referred to as information technology security. There is heavy dependence on processors in the IT industry that stock and communicate plenty of private and vital information about individuals. Therefore cybersecurity is a vital function, and it is required in almost all kinds of businesses.

Most Common Cybersecurity Threats

Computer threats are persistently ingenious. These are chiefs of disguise and alteration. These cyber-threats continually progress to discover new behaviors to aggravate, steal, and damage. Everyone should know the relevant material and resources needed to defend against difficult and increasing computer safety threats. In this way, individuals can stay safe while connected to the internet. Following are some common types of network and security threats:

- *Computer Viruses*

Everyone knows about computer viruses. For the most frequent Internet users, computer viruses are the greatest danger to cybersecurity. Computer viruses are sections of software programs that are intended to extend from one PC to another. Computer viruses are often showed as electronic mail attachments or transferred from particular websites with the intention of contaminating the computer. Computer viruses also have the capability of transferring to other computers on the contact list. Viruses are famous for showing themselves as spam. They can disable the security settings, damage the system, and take information from the computer, including private data such as PINs and passwords. They even have the capability of deleting the hard drive entirely.

• *Rogue Safety Software*

Hackers have found a new way of doing internet fraud. Rogue safety software is a malicious piece of software. It misguides the users into believing that there is a virus installed on their computer or their computer is not up to date. In both cases, these scammers offer them to download a piece of software on their computers. They sometimes ask for a specific amount to be paid too. The software that the users download is infected. In this way, the users are tricked into installing malicious software on their computers.

• *Trojan horses*

A Trojan horse is usually a malevolent piece of offensive program or software that hides behind any valid program. Users install it willingly without knowing about it. One of the ways in which they spread is by email. As soon as the user clicks the email, the Trojan horse is automatically downloaded in their system. Trojan horses also spread in the form of advertisements that are not genuine. Trojan horses have many capabilities that include stealing all the passwords in a computer, stealing sensitive and private information, and they can also track the webcams.

• *Spyware*

Spyware is similar in its working to adware. The spyware is installed on an individual's PC without his information. It can comprise of key loggers that keep track of individual data comprising of emails, PINs, debit, or credit card information. The most important risk associated with the use of spyware is Identity theft.

• *Computer Worms*

Computer worms are bits of malware software that duplicate rapidly and extend rapidly between computers. A worm extends from an infected PC by distributing itself to all the contacts of the computer; from there, this cycle continues until all of the computers are affected. The transmission of computer worms is often done by misusing software weaknesses.

• *Phishing Attack*

Phishing attacks include directed digital e-mails that are transferred to fool individuals into using a link. That link has the capability of installing malware and uncovering important data. Phishing attacks are getting more refined day by day. These kinds of cyber-attacks assist black hat hackers in taking user information regarding login credentials, credit card authorizations, and many types of private monetary information. These attacks also get information from private databases.

• *Ransomware*

In Ransomware, the hackers organize tools that permit them to steal a discrete database or establishment's databases accurately. After this, they keep all of the data under their control for ransom demands. The growth of cryptocurrencies, such as Bitcoin, is powering ransomware attacks by letting ransom demands to be funded secretly. Different businesses are continuing to emphasize the construction of resilient fortifications to protect against ransomware.

• *Crypto-jacking*

This is a relatively new term. It is introduced recently. Crypto-jacking is related to cryptocurrency. Crypto-jacking is a new trend that includes cybercriminals taking over the control of other people's home or work PCs to search for cryptocurrency. For utilizing the computing power for this purpose, the hackers use the computing resources of other individuals.

• *State Supported Attacks*

Entire nations are now consuming their cyber abilities to penetrate other managements. They implement attacks on other organizations. Cybersecurity is nowadays a major danger. It is not only a major danger for the private division and individuals, but it is also a danger for the administrations and countries as well.

• *IOT Attacks*

The Internet of Things is getting more universal by each passing day. It includes all the devices attached to the cloud. IOT includes connected electronic devices that are convenient for customers. Many businesses now utilize them to save currency by collecting huge quantities of perceptive information and reorganization of business procedures. The other side of IOT device usage is that more related devices mean larger danger. Therefore it makes IOT systems more susceptible to cyber-attacks and cyber threats. If hackers can gain access to IOT devices, these devices can be utilized to generate chaos, burden systems, and shut down important tools for monetary gain.

• *Third-party Risks*

Third parties, such as retailers and suppliers, pose an enormous danger to companies. Most of the businesses have no safe organizations or devoted groups in place to maintain this third-party personnel. Cyber offenders are becoming progressively refined, and cybersecurity dangers are increasing. The establishments are getting more and more alert of the risks that third parties pose.

• *Shortage of cybersecurity specialists*

Cyber-crime has intensified quickly in the past few years. Businesses and companies have struggled to appoint sufficient capable specialists to protect them against the rising threats. The great shortage of cybersecurity specialists remains to be a reason for fear. A robust and smart workforce is vital to battle the more recurrent and refined cybersecurity threats originating from all around the world.

• *Man in the Middle attacks*

Man-in-the-middle attacks are also sometimes known as "snooping attacks." They occur when an attacker is present between two-party dealings. In this attack, the hackers tap into other individual's networks and keep an eye on all the confidential transactions and gain access to private and financial information. The hackers set up fake Wi-Fi networks for individuals, or they sometimes install malware on the target's computer. The basic goal is the same. It is to gain valuable confidential information from individuals.

• *Obsolete hardware and software*

The hardware and software of a company should be latest and up-to-date. The latest hardware and software are necessary for the safety of the establishment's system, servers, electric devices, information, and clients. Obsolete technologies no longer offer protection against the latest cyber-attacks made by hackers and scammers. If the cybercriminals are inventing new strategies of hacking the systems and security, then there should be advanced hardware and software available for protection of the computers from unauthorized access.

● *Insufficient Patch Management*

Companies release software patches to deal with the weaknesses and vulnerabilities in the operating systems, computer programs, and other tools. Patch management is essential for the security of companies. If the software vulnerabilities are not covered properly, then they will leave holes in IT safety infrastructure. Preferably the process of patching must be applied as soon as a weakness is realized in software. The software liabilities leave the establishments at the risk of cyber-attacks, downtime, harm, and non-regulation in cybersecurity standards. Therefore patch management should be sufficient in order to keep the company away from the cyber-attacks.

● *Form Jacking*

This kind of cybersecurity danger includes a hacker taking control of forms on an eCommerce website. Most of the time, the cyber offenders make the use of a malevolent JavaScript program on the "forms page" usually present at the "Check out" page of the eCommerce websites. The main goal is to steal their client's monetary and expense data such as credit card numbers etc.

● *People as a cybersecurity threat*

Sometimes people are intended to harm a system, and sometimes people do it without any intention. Therefore individuals are a major danger to cybersecurity. These exposures come from workers, retailers, and anybody who can use the computer system within an organization. An information breach or cyber-attack can happen just because of a human mistake or a lack of cybersecurity responsiveness. Workers within an organization can be a substantial cybersecurity danger when they contemplate that they have something to get through their malevolent activities. Sometimes the people within an organization want to get the revenue by marketing or consuming the information they steal. Sometimes people want to get vengeance against a current or previous company for some alleged unfairness. These employers might install malware over the company's computers, download information, or execute other dangerous activities. In some cases, the personnel of retailers can also be considered as a potential risk.

Impacts of Cyber Attacks on Business

As technology is continuously developing, and the use of technology is growing, risk management has an essential part in safeguarding that such expertise does not expose businesses to cyber-attacks. Cyber-attacks can harmfully impact financial security and are now an intrinsic certainty that any maintainable business or industry must be prepared to face (Izuakor, 2016). A cyber-attack can cause a lot of harm to the business. Cyber-attack can affect business and customer reliance. The details of different kinds of impacts of cyber threats are as follows:

The financial cost of cyber-attack

Financial loss is considered as one of the most fundamental impacts of cyber-attacks. Financial loss can be considered as a backbone behind every cyber-attack. Usually, financial loss occurs from the stealing of business information, financial information, funds, and credit card information. One other cost that the businesses face from cyber-attacks is the cost to recover from a cyber-attack and the cost of repairing the systems.

Reputational Impact of a Cyber-Attack

Reliance is a vital component of customer association. Cyber-attacks can harm a business standing and impact the trust of the clients. This reputational impact can lead to the loss of clients, transactions, and incomes. The reputational impact of a cyber-attack can damage the trust between suppliers, investors, and partners within a business.

Legitimate Impact of a Cyber-Attack

Businesses have to defend the data. The confidentiality laws are required to maintain the safety of all individual data that is present. Within a business, this data can be about workers or clients. In some cases, if this information is unintentionally or purposely compromised, then the business has failed to install suitable safety actions, and it may have to face penalties and supervisory authorizations.

Psychological Impact of Cyber-Attack

The psychological impact affects the individuals responsible for maintaining cybersecurity within an organization. After a cyber-attack, the individuals feel unhappy, uncomfortable, disgraced, and confused as they consider the cyber-attack as their fault. This impact can be reduced by the proper training of individuals with the latest developments in mitigation strategies for cyber-attacks.

Physical Impact of a Cyber-Attack

The physical impact of a cyber-attack includes the damage to the physical infrastructure as a result of a cyber-attack. The common example of this impact is wiping off everything from the hard drive and leaving the hard drive entirely useless.

Social Impact of a Cyber-Attack

The social impact of a cyber-attack includes the disturbance to everyday life activities in an IT environment. It also includes the influence on key amenities, a harmful insight of technology, or descent in interior confidence within organizations that are affected by a cyber incident. The social impact of a cyber-attack affects business activities socially.

How can Cyber-Attacks be Reduced?

Cybersecurity breaks can upset even the strongest businesses. Therefore, it is tremendously vital to manage cybersecurity risks, consequently. In case if a cyber-attack occurs, an active "Cybersecurity event response strategy" must be present. This strategy will help businesses in:

- Reducing the effects of the cyber-attack.

- Reporting the cyber-attack incident to the reporting authority.

- Cleaning and recovering the effected computers and IT infrastructure after the cyber-attack.

- Recovering from the cyber-attack as soon as possible.

Many businesses become victims of cybersecurity attacks, and many businesses are at risk of cyber-attacks due to low-quality cyber-security plans. Here are some ways in which cybersecurity risk can be reduced within a business:

Creating responsiveness of cyber-security within an organization

Companies and Businesses can invest in great cybersecurity infrastructure, but in the end, it all comes in the hands of the employees who will practice the cyber-security practices. Companies have to rely on the employees for making the use of best practices regarding cyber-security. Every individual of the company should be trained properly regarding cybersecurity. Cyber-security education should be universal for every individual of the company. Some key points should be covered in this training. These key points include:

- Rules around satisfactory use of provided technology in both external and internal use.

- Procedure to safeguard that individual and business information is constantly safe from an external data breach.

- Measures on how cyber-attack recovery will be made on the occasion of a cyber-attack.

- Ensuring strong passwords for all the individuals ranging from people in the administration to the general staff.

- General and specific information on how workers are going to utilize the IT infrastructure, networks, and how their levels of access are defined within the organization.

- How to identify 'suspected' correspondences that the employees will receive during their normal working within an organization.

Investing in cyber safety and cyber-security backup

As the cyber-attacks are becoming more and more inventive every day, therefore the companies should invest in complex safety measures, vigorous backup options, and recovery arrangements to diminish risks associated with cyber-attacks. It is all about being practical and dropping the penalties of a cyber-attack. Investing in cyber-security measures is better than working on weak IT infrastructure with less protective measurements and undergoing extreme downtime or even paying a ransom for important information to be refunded.

Keeping up to date with all of the safety arrangements and testing the security measures regularly

Security systems should be updated regularly in order to keep the defenses up to date. In this way, the security defenses can deal with the current innovative hacking techniques. All of the IT infrastructures should be regularly updated. Consistent testing of the IT policy should be done to safeguard that the business is never left susceptible to a cyber-attack. The recovery plans should also be tested regularly to ensure proper safety.

Chapter Three

Cyber Technology

The war between cybersecurity professionals and black hat hackers is always continuous. This leads to an ever-developing chain of cybercrimes that continually overcome current cybersecurity technologies. The solution is present in the collective knowledge and the application of progressive cybersecurity skills. Black hat hackers are continuously finding new ways of stealing valuable information and getting money from hacking techniques. Businesses should work with the best practices of cyber technology in order to stay safe from malicious attacks. Identifying and establishing innovative cybersecurity plans to fight cyber threats is the requirement of the current cybersecurity situation. Here is the list of some emerging technologies that will be able to help businesses defend their IT infrastructures against external threats:

● *Hardware verification*

The failures of user credentials, such as names and passwords, are famous. There is a requirement of a more secure form of verification. A new method that is introduced in the use of authentication methods placed in the hardware. Some latest INTEL processors use this form of verification. These processors can syndicate a variation of hardware-enriched features to authenticate a user's distinctiveness. Good verification processes need three things from the end-users. These three things typically include a strong set of passwords, usernames, and typically a token, usually in the form of a security question. Hardware verification is especially important in the technical area of the "Internet of Things." In IOT technology, the network is important for the verifications of devices that connect to the cloud. Hardware authentication provides better cyber-security for cloud-based solutions.

• *User-conduct analytics*

This technology uses the concepts of big data. Cyber-experts keep a check on the user behavior. Whenever the behavior of compromised user credentials occurs, data scientists figure out that malevolent behavior is present. This method is based on differentiating legitimate users and fake users by utilizing their credentials. This method also uses the "peer analysis" techniques. Proper training for cyber-security specialists is essential for using the "User conduct analysis."

• *Preventing data damage*

Crucial technologies that prevent data damage are encryption and the use of tokens within IT processes. These techniques can protect the data on all levels. These techniques also provide a number of benefits, including no monetization of data in case of a successful data breach. Analytics on the data can be done in the data protected.

• *Deep learning skills*

Deep learning skills include a variety of technologies, such as the use of machine learning skills and concepts of artificial intelligence. These techniques primarily focus on the identification of irregular behavior. These techniques help in looking at business entities at all levels. Machine learning techniques can figure out malicious software behavior. Therefore machine-learning models can help in figuring out the malicious code.

• *Cloud technology*

The cloud technology has a transformative influence on security technology. Due to the introduction of cloud technology, different approaches to cloud security have appeared recently. On-premises methods will be transferred to the cloud. The cloud technology introduced the concepts of virtualized hardware, firewalls, and virtual interference detection mechanisms.

• *Blockchain cyber-security technology*

Blockchain cyber safety is one of the newest cyber safety expertise that is attaining recognition. The blockchain cyber technology works on the foundation of credentials among two business parties. Likewise, blockchain cyber safety works on the foundation of blockchain web essentials. Every follower in a blockchain is accountable for authenticating the legitimacy of the information that is added. Furthermore, blockchains generate a very resistant net for hackers, and it defends the information from being compromised. The usage of blockchain with the concepts of AI can create a vigorous authentication arrangement to keep probable cyber threats away.

• *Zero trust Models*

This Zero trust model of cyber safety is founded on a deliberation that a network is currently compromised. It enhances both types of interior and exterior securities in a network. The bottom line here is that together, both inner and outer networks are vulnerable to a hacking attack and need equivalent defense mechanisms. Zero trust models contain recognizing important business data, planning the movement of this information, rational or physical division, and control through mechanization and continuous checking.

Features that Must be Present in a Cyber Technology Platform

Features are the qualities that must be present in a cybersecurity platform. For an effective cyber technology platform, certain capabilities must be present in it to work efficiently and effectively. Following is the list of some features that a cyber technology must have:

- *Email security and web security must be covered*

According to statistics, at least 90% of cyber-attacks originate from phishing electronic mails, malevolent connections, or faulty URLs. A cybersecurity platform should apply strainers and check to these common dangerous vectors for obstructing malware and giving reflectiveness into irregular, distrustful, and malevolent actions.

- *Essential management over all the services*

Essential management means alignment organization and strategy organization, along with common management and reporting. Cyber technology platform organization delivers an accumulated substitute to the present condition where organizations function endpoint safety management, grid safety management, and malware management, etc.

- *Detection and prevention of Threats*

A cybersecurity technology platform must be equipped with detecting a cyber threat. After successful detection, it must be able to provide such functions that can terminate the threat process. In the last step, the cybersecurity platform must be able to roll back onto the original state of the system before the threat attack.

● *Cloud-based backend facilities*

The cloud can be considered as the backend intelligence of a cyber technology platform. Cloud-based facilities will collect doubtful behaviors across clients. These cloud-based facilities will track these behaviors through progressive and continually refining machine learning procedures. They will deliver tailored analytics and risk intelligence for specific clients and businesses. Therefore, all the clients will benefit from general and tailored services offered by the cloud.

● *Open API connection support*

Cybersecurity platforms must be equipped with APIs for third-party skill incorporation and developer assistance. This will also reassure the network result where cyber safety technology platform operators share development's finest practices. In this way, cybersecurity experts can make custom solutions by using third party APIs according to their demands.

● *A technology platform that offers numerous deployment choices*

Big establishments incline to use hybrid cyber technology placements. They usually run the security applications at business headquarters while choosing for cloud-based safety representation services to assist distant workplaces and mobile workforces. Cybersecurity skill platforms will provide hybrid provision over all the safety panels with a central organization plan.

Best Cybersecurity Practices for Businesses

The small-sized businesses are primary targets of cybercriminals. In reality, small-sized businesses get attacked by hackers more often than large-sized businesses. According to the statistics, in the US, 71 percent of cyber-attacks occurred at businesses with fewer than 100 workers (Segal, 2019). Small-sized businesses have more security breaches than large-sized businesses. All kinds of cyber-attacks usually have 3 main types of purposes. These purposes include stealing personal data, getting money, and stealing user credentials. Small size companies have fewer safe networks. Therefore it makes it easier to break the network security. Automated attacks initialized by hackers can breach a number of networks automatically. The network security within a business, irrespective of its size, is immensely important. Within small-sized businesses, an insufficient amount of time, money, and lack of cybersecurity specialists is a top reason for cyber-attacks. Here is a list of some best cyber security practices for all kinds of businesses. These security practices will save the companies from the hacker attacks and unwanted access to their monetary data and sensitive information. The detail of these practices is as follows:

- *Utilizing a firewall for business*

The primary defense mechanism for a cyber-attack is the firewall. This is the first layer of security that is attacked by hackers. Setting up a proper firewall for your network means that there is a defense mechanism staying between sensitive information and cyber hackers. Currently, along with the typical exterior firewall, many businesses are beginning to set up interior firewalls to deliver extra defense. Workers of a company who work remotely must also install firewalls on their computer systems so that the data of the company will always be secure.

● *Documenting the cyber safety guidelines and policies*

Regarding the field of cybersecurity, every company and business should properly document the policies and procedures. Documentation of all the security protocols is essential. Different types of software are available in the market for documenting the protocols. This software typically includes cybersecurity portals and voluntary cybersecurity programs for businesses.

● *Proper planning for mobile devices that are used within a company*

With the growing fame of wearable gadgets, such as smart tablets, televisions, watches, and health trackers with wireless competence, it is vital to add all of these devices in a cybersecurity procedure. The automatic security updates must be enabled along with strong password security measures that are required on every remote device that accesses the company's network.

● *Proper cybersecurity training for all the employees*

Every employee who works within a business must be capable of using cybersecurity protocols defined by the company. Proper training is essential for individuals to save themselves from cyber threats. Proper updates should be available on the newer versions of the security protocols within a company.

● *Secure software practices*

Many data breaches occur due to stolen and weak passwords set by company individuals. Any device that accesses the company's network must be password protected. Passwords must be enforced using strong policies, including capital letters, small letters, and special characters.

● *Recurrently back up for the company information*

Backing up all the data deposited on the cloud is essential. It is necessary to ensure that backups are collected in a distinct site in case of fire or natural disaster. Recurrently creating backups is essential to safeguard that there will always be the latest backup always available. It is also important to have a functioning backup all the time.

● *Using anti-malware software*

Regardless of all the security measures that a company takes, a security mistake made by an employee can cripple the entire company's system. Anti-malware software must be installed on the computers so that whenever a phishing link is clicked by a worker by mistake, a defending mechanism is present. Phishing specific tactics are covered by anti-malware software. Therefore for preventing phishing attacks, anti-malware software must be installed on the company's systems.

● *Using Multifactor Identification methods*

Utilizing the multi-factor identification option on the main network and electronic mail products is easy. It also provides an extra layer of protection. Cybersafety is an important target. Cyber offenders get more progressive each day. For the protection of the company's data as much as imaginable, it is very vital that each and every worker take cybersecurity the highest precedence.

• *Protection of the information*

Cyber offenders can generate correspondence addresses and web applications that look genuine. Hackers can forge caller ID materials. Scammers can even take over business's social media accounts and send apparently genuine mails. Therefore, it is significant not to lose your business's information, delicate evidence, or knowledgeable property. Take this example; if an employee shares an image on the web that demonstrates a whiteboard or processer display in the background, this picture can unintentionally disclose statistics that somebody exterior to the business should not get. A business can defend its personnel, clients, and information by generating and allocating corporate strategies that will use subjects such as "how to abolish information that is not desirable" and "how to recognize and report doubtful correspondences or malware.

• *Only a secure WIFI connection should be accepted*

Workplace Wi-Fi nets must be safe, encoded, and concealed. If a worker is working remotely, the worker can help to protect the data by using a simulated remote network, if the business is using a VPN connection. A VPN is vital while doing work in the external environment of the office or on a corporate journey. Community Wi-Fi nets can be dangerous and make your information at risk of being interrupted. A good and safe version of a VPN connection must be ensured at the workplace.

• *Investing in Cybersecurity systems*

Minor industries might hesitate while anticipating the price of capitalizing in a superior safety organization. That typically comprises of defenses such as robust malware and antivirus discovery, exterior hard drives that are responsible for back up information, and successively running steady arrangement checks. Making this kind of investment initially could protect businesses and personnel from the probable monetary and lawful expenses of being breached.

It is significant for a business to deliver data safety in the office. In the case of a security breach, the IT section or Information Safety manager should be informed that a security problem might be present. There might be a fault in the IT organization that the business needs to cover or fix. The earlier a company can report a problem, the better it will be for the safety of the company.

● *Enforcing Biometric Security*

Biometrics safeguards fast verification, safe contact organization, and exact worker checking.

Confirming users' individualities before giving access to valued possessions is essential for companies. Voice acknowledgment, impression examinations, hand biometrics, facial credit, social biometrics, and posture analysis are flawless choices to classify whether or not the users are genuine and legitimate. Utilizing biometrics delivers more safe verification than passwords and SMS confirmation. Due to all of these reasons, biometric authentication is an important method of user verification. Verification is not the one used for biometrics. Safety managers get benefits from a wide variety of biometric-based gears that permit them to notice hacked and compromised private accounts in the actual amount of time.

There is another field within Biometrics, and it is called "Behavioral Biometrics." Behavioral biometrics examines the methods by which workers interrelate with the input machines. If irregular conduct is noticed, a device directs a caution warning to safety managers so that they can respond instantly. Different types of Behavioral Biometrics can be placed within a business's IT infrastructure. This Behavioral Biometrics will include the followings:

o *Keyboard dynamics:*

The keyboard dynamics reflect the typing quickness and the inclination to make distinctive errors indefinite words for generating the end user's performance outlines.

o *Mouse Dynamics:*

The mouse dynamics measure the amount of time among ticks, beat, and grace of pointer drive.

o *Eye Biometrics:*

The eye biometrics practices the eye and stare tracking strategies to measure videos of eye association and notice eye patterns.

According to the statistics, the development of the biometrics marketplace increased from $16.8 billion in 2018 to an estimated $41.8 billion by 2023 (12 Best Cybersecurity Practices in 2019, 2019). Therefore, investing in the best cyber biometric cybersecurity practices is the best option for cyber companies.

● *Using a risk-based approach for security purposes*

Risk assessment is the best tool for companies to assess their risks. Every business has its own particular and concealed risks, so concentrating on compliance and conforming to all the typical guidelines are enough to defend the delicate information. A risk assessment should cover the important assets of the company, the current status of the cybersecurity, and the management of cybersecurity within a company. Appropriate risk calculation permits the company to evade lots of disagreeable things such as penalties for failing to conform to guidelines, remediation charges for possible leakages, security breaches, and the damages from lost or incompetent processes. Adjustments in a company should be made after identifying the weak spots within the cybersecurity practices. A keen eye should be kept on the hacking attempts at all times. Worksheets for risk assessment are also very important for the company's risk assessment.

• *Management of the IOT Devices*

The most puzzling mechanism about IOT devices is their entree to subtle and sensitive information. All of the IOT devices are potential access points for hackers and scammers. For example, a conceded printer can permit malicious hackers and scammers to get the view of all papers that are passed through the printer or scanned by the printer. Following are some of the business security's best practices:

- o Doing the penetration testing for the analysis of real-time risks and planning the safety strategies according to the requirements.

- o Encryption strategies must be enforced for all kinds of data.

- o Authentication for only giving the connection to the verified endpoints.

- o Proper credentials should be followed for every end-user.

o The latest router should be installed along with a proper firewall.

o A scalable safety IT infrastructure should be available for all the departments with the company.

o Proper endpoint security mechanisms should be installed over the entire business's IT infrastructure.

● *Giving users fewer privileges*

There should not be too many privileged users in any business. Allowing fresh employees all privileges automatically permits them to contact the sensitive information even if they don't essentially require it. It raises the risk of inner cyber threats and permits scammers to get entree to delicate information whenever any of the new worker's account is hacked. The rule of least privilege is to be always followed. The company should assign every new account the least privileges possible and escalate privileges if necessary.

The Future of Cyber Security

Whenever a user connects to the web from a processer or phone, there is a rising danger of cyber-attack and cyber-threats. If the danger is aimed at a user's workplace, then the whole business around could become susceptible too. A good company, irrespective of its scope or worldwide reach, should ultimately recognize that cybersecurity needs substantial investment.

Many experts consider that an innovative cyber technology founded on the concepts of machine knowledge and AI (Artificial Intelligence) is the future of cyber-technology when it comes to processer, network, and information security. Nowadays, businesses place importance on the safety of their interior systems. If scammers and hackers accomplish to penetrate the network layer of their organization, within a less amount of time, a "minor" break can become a significant hacking attack.

A common method for network defense is a strong firewall. Firewalls can be present either as a software technique or a hardware method that is actually linked with the network. In both of these cases, the firewall's work is to monitor which web connections are permitted on which ports. The firewall also has the function of blocking all other irrelevant requests. A server administrator is typically responsible for managing these policies regarding firewalls. In a scenario where a hacker has bypassed the firewall and net safety, a business's succeeding line of protection is the antivirus software that is intended to scan hardware and software for malevolent code. The aim is to eliminate the malware before it can distribute itself to other machinery and issue a kind of attack such as ransomware.

In the case of cybersecurity, there is no technique present that is more valued than the training of the workforce regarding cybersecurity. The effective establishments run training sessions on a consistent basis for fresh and existing employees to teach them about threats that exist online and methods in which they can defend themselves and the business.

How AI (Artificial Intelligence) will shape the future of Cyber Security Methodologies

The popular cybersecurity techniques and tools need human communication or configuration at all the levels of cybersecurity. For example, an individual belonging to an IT Team has to fix the firewall strategies and backup timetable. It is the duty of this individual to ensure that everything is running smoothly according to set policies. The progression in the field of Artificial Intelligence will change this entire equation.

In the near future, businesses will be capable of trusting on clever techniques to deal with the bulk of occasion monitoring and event reactions. The succeeding technology of firewalls will have built-in machine learning tools. These tools will permit the software to identify designs in net requests and robotically block those designs that could be a potential risk or danger to the business.

Specialists also believe that the ordinary language abilities of "Artificial Intelligence" can play a large part in the future of cyber safety techniques. The philosophy is that by skimming big portions of information across the network, AI arrangements can study how cyber-attacks initiate and the AI arrangements can propose answers for cybersecurity specialists within the business.

Security services and products constructed on the AI structure are quite expensive. This high price of such sophisticated systems can pose a dilemma for small-sized and medium-sized companies currently. Appointing and associating a team of machine-learning specialists to shape custom cybersecurity resolutions might not be an instant or even near future selection. Currently, it is highly favorable to invest in hybrid techniques and tools that are present in the marketplace, and implant AI expertise in human functioned products and services.

The mainstream internet users generate their own modified passwords for every website or facility that they contribute to over the internet. This structure can be tiring to preserve, and it is susceptible to cyber-attacks if the users trust easy passwords or utilize the old passwords for numerous sites.

There have been developments in the performance of PIN manager software in current years. Most of this software aims to streamline and fortify online security. This software eliminates a big share of manual exertion from the job through procedures that propose and stock passwords difficult enough to decrease the user's chances of being hacked by hackers. The concepts of artificial intelligence could introduce a new internet world without any passwords. New developments in the world of identity management propose that one day, PINs and passwords might essentially be substituted by intelligent AI-based systems. In this new technology, Artificial Intelligence concepts would track every operator within a business based on roles, rights, and mutual activities. Any abnormality from the standard practices would be identified, and it will need the individual to use an additional kind of verification, such as biometrics, that creates the scans of facial structures and fingerprints.

Financing in cybersecurity resolutions and techniques is an essential job for companies of all kinds, regardless of the size of the company. Businesses with lesser finances may think they can save cash by taking shortcuts, but in reality, they are frequently the major objective for hackers as their cybersecurity defenses are weak. Cybersecurity services prove their value by decreasing the organization's danger and defending it from risky hackers. Now due to progressions in AI technologies, businesses will have no requirement of maintaining large cyber safety teams inside their IT section as in the future, the majority of the tasks regarding cyber-security will be handled by AI processes.

Gears founded on machine learning are very effective at picking up on designs and discovering malicious events before a human can typically recognize. For the current situation, the establishments should train the workers with the advanced tools and techniques in implementing a cybersecurity plan and keep a keen eye on the latest AI developments.

Based on the above-mentioned evidence, it can be presumed that the future of cybersecurity lies in the hands of the latest Artificial Intelligence concepts. By using advanced AI systems, the entire processing abilities of cybersecurity technologies will be modified. It will also provide numerous benefits to the companies and businesses of all sizes.

Chapter Four

Analytics and
Metrics for Big Data

Analytics include the analysis and decision making the capability of a system. The metrics include the measurement of performance and the measurement of progress within a company. The metrics provide vital performance pointers. Metrics give the answer to the "what" kind of questions, and the analytics give the answer to "So what" kind of questions. This section will provide a detailed insight into the analytics and metrics of big data, Data Science, and Cybersecurity.

Analytics and Metrics of Big Data and Data Science

Big data analytics is a very composite procedure of inspecting big and diverse data groups and information to expose material such as concealed designs, unidentified associations, marketplace tendencies, and customer favorites that can assist establishments in making knowledgeable corporate choices.

In an overall sense, data analytics skills and techniques deliver a means to examine data groups and draw deductions about the given information, which will help establishments in making knowledgeable business choices. Data analysis provides solutions for elementary questions regarding business processes and

.esentation. Big data analytics is a procedure of progressive analytics, which includes composite requests with features such as analytical models, arithmetical procedures, and what-if investigation motorized by high-presentation analytics organizations.

Big data analytics are determined by particular analytic arrangements and software along with highly efficient computing schemes; big data analytics provides numerous business benefits. Some of these benefits are as follows:

- Innovative revenue occasions.

- Highly effective advertising.

- Improved client provision.

- Better working competence.

- Competitive benefits over competitors.

Big data analytics requests authentication of big data forecasters, data experts, analytical modelers, mathematicians, and other analytics specialists to examine rising capacities of organized business information. These experts can also analyze other kinds of information that are frequently left unused by predictable Business intelligence operations and analytical processes.

Data analytics work in this way that Hadoop bunches and NoSQL organizations are utilized chiefly as staging parts for big data before it is sent into a data warehouse or logical database for analytical processing. The data typically processed is in a précised format. This format is more beneficial to relational constructions. When the data is complete, it can be examined with the software normally used for progressive analytic procedures.

Text excavating and arithmetical analysis software also play a great role in the big data analytics process. This software has the capability of mainstreaming business intelligence data and providing data conception gears.

Data scientists use many performance metrics, such as Correctness, memory, accuracy, understanding, etc. Data scientists use performance metrics using pictures so that anyone can understand the predictive models. The most important performance metric used for evaluating the performance is accuracy. This metric describes the model's accuracy to predict a situation. Another performance metric is known as precision. This metric shows the precision of the results in a specific situation. The sensitivity performance metric describes the sensitive content within a model. The specificity performance metric shows the specific criteria in the given information. These 4 performance metrics are used in the field of big data to describe the predictive models for predictive analysis accurately.

Cybersecurity Analytics and Metrics

Establishments currently face a broader range and a larger occurrence of cyber threats. These cyber-threats include all kids of APTs (advanced persistent threats), cyber conflict, unrestrained occurrences via botnet programs, malevolent scripts, malware attacks, which are as-a-service through the Dark Net, or even interior threat occurrences from persons within the business and organization. The whole thing that includes dispersed denial of service attacks (DDoS), man-in-the-middle cyber-attacks, phishing attacks, crypto-jacking, ransomware, and data breaches hit industries of all dimensions and in all businesses continually and every day.

Security Analytics is a method that is used in cybersecurity. It is fixated on the examination of information to create practical security actions. As an example, observed system traffic could be utilized to recognize pointers of hacking attempts before a real danger happens. Any business, no matter what the type, cannot forecast the future of the company. In case of safety threats, arranging and installing security analytics techniques that are able to examine safety actions can notice a cyber threat before it has an opportunity to affect the IT organization.

The arena of cyber safety analytics is rising. This field is full of prospects, and it offers a vigorous resolution for establishments that are looking to stay away from susceptibilities. The cybersecurity field makes these organizations stay one step ahead of the hackers and scammers. A number of factors are involved in the increasing demand for security analytics. Some of these factors are as follows:

- *Moving between protection and detection*
Scammers use a varied range of cyber-attack tools that achieve numerous susceptibilities. Some cyberthreats can go unnoticed for many months. Safety analytics gears can keep track of mutual danger designs and send warnings the instant an irregularity is exposed.

- *A cohesive view of the business*
Security analytics arranges data in a way that it proposes both actual time and past view of actions. This analytic

technique delivers an integrated vision of threats and safety breaks from a crucial point of view and permits for keener development, quicker determination, and better choice-making ability.

- ***Seeing effects and a reoccurrence on investment***
There is rising stress on IT teams to convey the results to high-ranking management and investors. Security analytics delivers results in less time for resolving the metrics and less false positives that permit analysts to classify threats and reply to safety breaks rapidly.

One of the main advantages of cybersecurity analytics is the sheer capacity and variety of data that can be examined in less time according to the requirements. This information typically includes the following types of data:

- End user's behavioral information.

- Information regarding Net traffic.

- Information about business applications and enterprise applications.

- Cloud traffic data.

- Non-IT infrastructure's data.

- Peripheral threat intellect bases.

- Access and individual organization information.

- Proof of agreement during a review.

By examining such a wide variety of information, establishments are able to attach the dots among numerous alerts and actions simply. The outcomes are active security event discoveries and quicker reply times that assist the corporate to defend the reliability of organizations and information. Security analytics techniques also contribute the amenability with business and administration documentations. Rules such as PCI-DSS and HIPAA need organizations to observe information actions and record information collection for forensics and reviewing dedications (What is Security Analytics?).

Security analytics can be applied for a varied diversity of use cases, from operator performance checking to network transportation analysis. A few common examples of use cases are as follows:

- Examining network traffic to notice designs that designate a possible attack.

- Checking employer behavior, particularly possibly doubtful behavior.

- Noticing insider pressures.

- Noticing information exfiltration.

- Classifying accounts that may have been negotiated.

In a domain where downtime due to any hacking attempt can cause disasters, establishments are required to consider more vigorous, dependable, and responsive methods of danger detection.

Operative management of variable presentation catalogs in IT safety can mean the variance between a real-world and well-organized project and a comprehensive money wastage. In cybersecurity, it is an emerging training to track cyber safety metrics. You cannot manage something if you cannot measure it properly. Cybersecurity metrics are a significant method of keeping track of security efforts. Good cybersecurity metrics are required for efficient and effective communication with business stakeholders. Cybersecurity metrics provide key performance indicators, which are vital for measuring the performance of the cybersecurity practices within an organization. Metrics also give an insight over how the services of cybersecurity are improved over a period of time. The metrics should be very clear and relevant to cybersecurity information. This will help even the non-technical individuals within the company to understand the cybersecurity situation effectively. Some key performance indicator examples are as follows:

● *Level of preparation*
This includes the number of devices that are attached to the network. How many devices are fully patched and currently up to date with respect to performance?

● *Anonymous devices on the interior network*
The workforces carry their devices at work. The company might also be utilizing the Internet of Things (IoT) services. These are enormous dangers for businesses as these devices are possibly not secure and safe from hacking attempts.

● *Interruption attempts from hackers*
It will include the list of a number of attempts in which hackers have tried to break the company's networks?

• *Number of days required to patch*

Will it track the record of a number of days required by an IT team to apply the security patches? Hackers and scammers often achieve delays between patch issues and the application of patches.

• *How many cyber incidents are reported properly*

Are the workers reporting cybersecurity problems to the IT team within the business? It is a worthy sign. This reporting of cyber issues signifies that the workforces and other shareholders identify cyber issues. This also implies that the cyber training provided to the employees in a company is working.

The cybersecurity metrics that a company will select will be determined by the organization's requirements and its level of risks. Metrics should be clear to anyone who will read the report. The cybersecurity metrics should define the organization's security to the business frontrunners. By monitoring the cybersecurity of the entire business, best cybersecurity decisions can be made regarding the company in the future. The following are some cybersecurity metrics that can be utilized for tracking to safeguard the competence of the safety developments.

• *For any hacking attempt, the meantime to attack and respond*

The poor performance of a company regarding the detection and response of a hacking attempt impacts the company greatly. This impact can be in the form of huge costs required to get back on point from the attack. For any IT security infrastructure, these two factors are very vital. It is necessary for a business to train their company's individuals accordingly for the detection of these two factors.

● *A variety of systems with recognized susceptibilities*

Knowing the variety of susceptible properties in the IT setting is an important cybersecurity metric to defining the risk that your corporate experiences. Handling updates and software patches is a multipart procedure, but it is very significant to evade ambiguities that can be misused in the IT settings. A susceptibility scan that comprises of all the assets will designate what requests are to be completed in order to progress the safety stance of the business. A susceptibility management package is a necessity in the current situation.

● *SSL credentials configured wrongly*

An SSL certificate is a small-sized folder that confirms the possession of a cryptographic key to the web application or business. The data is being switched with these web applications and businesses, and it assures the genuineness of the business. Checking the safety provisions for each certificate while safeguarding that they are correctly configured on IT systems, stops them from getting into the hands of the criminals. In this way, the business's digital individuality cannot be utilized to take end user's data.

● *Amount of data relocated using the business network*

If your company personnel have unobstructed access to the web through the business network, then checking the capacity of network transportation permits businesses to recognize misappropriation of company possessions. When downloading software, cassettes, pictures, and requests, a user has a chance of encountering the botnets and malware to attack their IT settings.

This chance increases greatly if the transfers are from websites that are famous and recognized as dangerous for malware attacks.

● *Users with a high level of access*

Finest practices in data security organization comprise of complete control of an employee's level of access to business resources. It is essential for a worker only to get the information, IT arrangements, and properties that are obligatory to their own work. Recognizing the access levels of all net operators permits the company to regulate them as desirable by delaying any other user or manager that does not require the company's network.

● *Days required to neutralize previous employee's credentials*

By checking these cybersecurity metrics, a company can describe whether the Human Possessions and IT players are working correctly or not. In a perfect situation, the access of operators that are terminated from the business must be disregarded directly. If the credentials of such employees are active, then it is an incredible danger. It can lead to the loss of important company information, and the devices of the company can be hijacked and compromised from obsolete accounts.

● *Checking the communication ports that are opened for connection purposes*

Inbound traffic should not be allowed. Outbound connections should be checked regularly to ensure that the traffic is moving swiftly or not. All the protocols responsible for remote access must be checked regularly to ensure the total protection of the company's assets.

- *Checking the third party access levels regularly*

Sometimes third parties are given access by the company's personnel to complete a project in a given amount of time. It is vital to ensure that after granting access and completing the task, the service of remote access is terminated or not. If the remote access is not terminated on time, then it can pose a great risk as the third party can come back without any alert or warning, and they can steal important data as well. Therefore all the third party accesses must be blocked after the use of service.

- *The proportion of corporate partners with efficient cybersecurity strategies*

There should be a strong control and monitoring of the cybersecurity metrics of the corporations that offer facilities for businesses. Providing access to the company's IT infrastructures to the outsourced corporations can be an enormous danger if it does not have operational policies for its own security first.

Conclusion

The volume of big data at present is enormous. This volume is predicted to rise exponentially as innovative technologies such as the more universal IOT gadgets, drones, and devices, which are a wearable increase in use. According to research, 90 % of the big data in the current IT world has been produced in the last two years (Buttice, 2019). The current progressions in deep learning are playing an important part in assisting businesses to make use of this valuable data. Big data and corporate analytics solutions are considered as a major technology innovation currently. The digital IT processes are further built on the advanced concepts of Artificial intelligence and automation processes.

Big data specialists make the connection between raw information and practical data. Data specialists must have the ability to operate data on the deepest stages. Their knowledge should enable them to understand the data's tendencies and designs in numerous different procedures. The computer programming languages and methods used to attain these objectives are increasing in forte and statistics. Inside a business, data scientists help to resolve big data issues, but typically these issues may be vague. To more confuse the subject, some data specialists work externally to any particular group. One common example of this scenario is the academic research-based field. Big Data Analytics is a security improving device of the future. The quantity of data that can be collected, prepared, and used for the employers in a modified fashion would take a lot of processing time.

Establishments are sinking with the huge volumes of data, and it appears that the businesses need to transfer to completely algorithmic information-driven forecasts to live in an extremely competitive IT domain. This situation makes the challenge of clever usage of these enormous quantities of fresh information. High level and better performance-based predictive analytic models are required for modeling the big data projects. After identification of an issue worth resolving with predictive analytics. It is essential to consult with advisers who make predictive analysis models. A predictive model has four basic stages of solving a problem. These 4 stages include management, planning, delivery, and operation on the problem, along with all of the risk factors that are involved in the whole process.

Data science is a versatile arena that utilizes technical approaches, procedures, processes, and arrangements to mine information and understandings from organized and unorganized information. The main benefit of data science over outdated measurements is that it could create deductions from a garbage pile of the allegedly unconnected data. In the field of data science, the data experts will play with procedures and algorithms for utilizing their understandings and creatively to improve the arithmetical model. A thorough understanding of the business procedures is mandatory for the data scientists to perform data science methodologies. The profession of data science will increase competence, efficiency, and output within businesses and companies. Data science contributes to the discovery of the data insights and the development and progress of data products. Both of these factors will greatly increase business value. Increasing business value is the optimum goal of the data science field.

Establishments are discovering themselves under the burden to respond rapidly to the vigorously growing number of cybersecurity dangers. Cyber threat management strategies are mandatory nowadays for businesses to defend themselves against external threats. The susceptibility organization life cycle is intended to counter the struggles made by the invaders in the fastest and most operative way. Cyber-security complications arise from the intrinsic nature of the IT infrastructure. Complex IT systems and the nature of human judgment all contribute to determining the level of cyber-attack. Threats to cyber-security progress and evolve continuously. The hackers and scammers continuously invest in new techniques to hack the organizations and businesses for material gains. There are typically three things for which hacking attempts are made. These three things include User credentials, the company's valuable information, and monetary gains. The monetary gains are usually the prime factors that influence hacking attempts. Cybersecurity defenses for a company are an ongoing process. The security procedures are continually getting advance. As the hackers continually adopt new strategies, therefore the defenders of the companies known as white hat hackers must also frequently use new techniques for effective defense of the company's information. Best cybersecurity practices must be followed for a safe system and up to date system free from all kinds of cyberattacks.

IT Analytics include the examination and choice-making competence of an IT system. The metrics comprise the extent of performance and the dimension of development and progress within a business. Regarding the big data, data analytics services and methods provide a way to inspect information collections and draw inferences about the specified data, which will support establishments in making well-informed business decisions. Data scientists use many different kinds of performance metrics for evaluating the performance of the company. Data scientists make the use of performance metrics by consuming graphical techniques such as pictures. Graphical representation makes it easy to comprehend the predictive models. The most vital performance metric utilized for assessing the performance of a business in big data is accurate.

Cybersecurity analytics is based on the inspection of data to create real-world security actions. The outcome of cybersecurity analytics is vigorous safety occasion detection and earlier response times. Both of these factors help the business to protect and guard the consistency of organizations. Security analytic techniques also assist in the responsiveness of business and management credentials.

The cybersecurity metrics will be determined by the security risks and cybersecurity situation of the company. The cybersecurity metrics for any organization must be clear and consistent for anyone to understand. Some important metrics for cybersecurity include the time of the attack for a hacking attempt and the meantime to respond, third party access levels, the time required to recover from a cyber-attack, third party access levels, etc. Every business should always be prepared for external cyber-attacks, and appropriate mitigation strategies should be present to neutralize the threats.

Bibliography

12 Best Cybersecurity Practices in 2019. (2019, May 30). Retrieved from ekransystem.com: https://www.ekransystem.com/en/blog/best-cyber-security-practices

Big data Basics. (n.d.). Retrieved from sisense.com: https://www.sisense.com/glossary/big-data-basics/

Buttice, C. (2019). Big Data for Big (and Small) Business.

Data Science and Its Growing Importance. (n.d.). Retrieved from https://www.educba.com: https://www.educba.com/data-science-and-its-growing-importance/

Izuakor, C. (2016). Understanding the Impact of Cyber Security Risks on Safety. *2nd International Conference on Information Systems Security and Privacy.*

L, A. B. (2019). Top 8 programming languages every data scientist should master in 2019.

Methews, K. (2019). Why Data Science is The Career of The Future.

Segal, C. (2019). 8 Cyber Security Best Practices For Your Small To Medium-Size Business.

Thompson, R. (n.d.). Understanding Data Science and Why It's So Important. *Behind the data.*

Vaidya, N. (2019, May 22). Data Science vs Big Data vs Data Analytics. p. 1.

What is Security Analytics? (n.d.). Retrieved from Forcepoint.com: https://www.forcepoint.com/cyber-edu/security-analytics

Made in the USA
Middletown, DE
28 May 2021